Starting to Paint Portraits

Starting to Paint Portraits
Bernard Dunstan

Studio Vista   London

Watson-Guptill Publications   New York

Acknowledgements

Portraits used in this book are reproduced by kind permission of:
Kyffin Williams Esq (p. 73)
Peter Greenham Esq (p. 77)
Richard Lee Esq (p. 79)
Josef Herman Esq (p. 80)
E. R. P. Wilson Esq (p. 83)
Mr and Mrs Eric Conrad (p. 85)
The Governors of Warwick School (p. 93)

General Editors Janey O'Riordan and Brenda Herbert
© Bernard Dunstan 1966
Published in London by Studio Vista Limited
Blue Star House, Highgate Hill, London N 19
and in New York by Watson-Guptill Publications
165 West 46th Street, New York 10036
Reprinted 1967, 1969
Library of Congress Catalog Card Number 66–13006
Set in Folio Grotesque 8 and 9 pt.
Printed and bound in Great Britain by
Bookprint Limited, Crawley, Sussex

SBN: 289. 27998. 4

Contents

Introduction

This book is not about a special kind of painting. There is no difference between a portrait and any other kind of objective painting - still life or landscape, for example - in terms of technique or method. The problems we face are exactly the same: to analyse what we see, and to put down an equivalent to it in terms of paint.

So we will not be discussing any specialised methods of painting; no dodges or tricks are involved. The purpose of this book is to get away from set methods and recipes, as far as that is possible, and to attempt instead to show you ways of finding things out for yourself, and of evolving your own style.

Though a portrait is essentially only a picture which happens to have a person as its subject, we do imply in our use of the word an attempt to capture as closely as possible the character of the sitter - to 'get a likeness', in fact. Otherwise we would talk about a painting of a head or a figure, rather than a portrait. It is here that we find the main distinction between this and other kinds of painting.

A painter needs a certain temperament to do good portraits. He must be interested in other people, get on well with them, and be prepared to adapt his methods - his speed of working, particularly - to the situation. Besides trying to paint a good picture, he has to deal all the time with another human being. You are not likely to paint good portraits unless you can do this.

No book can give you much help here. But the fact that you are reading this book presumably means that you have the necessary interest in people. We will be dealing later with the more specialised aspects of portraiture - likeness, and so on - but for the moment I think we should concentrate on the fundamental problems of drawing and painting, which are going to come up whatever style you may wish to paint in.

As I work almost entirely in oil, I will necessarily be dealing mostly with that medium, though I shall touch briefly on other methods. So perhaps we should start by considering the essential materials of the painter.

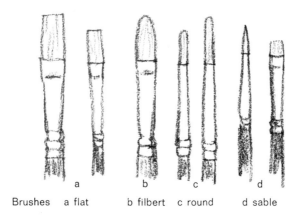

Brushes   a flat   b filbert   c round   d sable

1 Materials

Painting is quite hard enough as it is, and you must get every help you can from the tools of your craft. Poor quality materials will make it impossible to do good work. There are three essentials: good brushes, good colours, and a satisfactory support to paint on. Let us take these three items separately.

Brushes

A good brush is one that is flexible and clean, and comes to a proper shape naturally. The bristles should not be too short. The square, stubby brushes that you still see around are quite untraditional; they were mainly used about the turn of the century. Avoid them - they tend to give a very mechanical and monotonous touch. A good brush does not merely make a mark of a certain thickness: it should also be possible to draw freely with it.

    Painting a head is, as I have said, no different from painting anything else; but perhaps more than any other subject, it needs flexibility and precision of touch. You are going to have to establish smallish forms with some accuracy, and this means drawing with the paint the whole time.

Brush marks

Brushes that are flexible and fairly long haired, whether flat, round or filbert (see illustration), are the only sort with which you can draw as well as lay patches of colour. A flat brush can be turned on its side, and is capable of considerable delicacy of touch.

As well as these hog hair (or bristle) brushes, you should also have one or two pointed sables.

Good quality brushes should keep their shape well, but no brush will be much good for long unless it is treated well. They must be washed at the end of each·day's painting.

Keep a jam jar filled with turps substitute by you. Use it for washing the brushes out while you are painting, and when you have finished work for the day, clean them in it thoroughly, dry them on a rag, and then complete the cleaning with soap and water. Hold the soap in one hand and rub the brushes over it, then clean them carefully with the palm of the hand and the fingers. Finish by rinsing in water before shaping the bristles with the fingers and putting them away carefully. The whole operation need only take a few minutes, and should never on any account be missed. If you remember in the middle of the night that you have left your palette and brushes uncleaned, get up and do it!

You won't need a large quantity of brushes, though most painters do collect a fairly big stock. Even then, they probably have no more than half a dozen favourite ones going at a time. Old worn ones are still useful for scrubbing in large areas of paint in the preliminary stages of covering a canvas - an operation which, if the canvas is rough, can wear down a new brush very quickly.

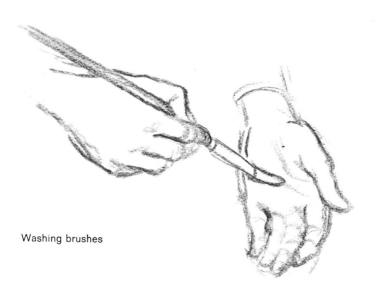

Washing brushes

Colours

There is little to say here. All the oil colours on the market are much the same in quality, and any of the grade called 'artist's colours' will be suitable. Everyone develops their own likes and dislikes, and their own pet palette, but you could start with a range such as this, all of which are permanent:

Flake White	Burnt Sienna
Cadmium Yellow Light	Raw Umber
Yellow Ochre	Ultramarine
Raw Sienna	Cobalt Blue
Permanent or Cadmium Red	Viridian
Crimson Alizarin	Ivory Black

Other colours can be added to this list. Don't be too conservative; if you like the look of a colour, buy a tube and see if it is useful to you. You should check on the manufacturer's list to see that it is permanent.

Put out the colours on your palette in the same rational order every time, so that you know where they are as instinctively as a pianist knows the notes on the keyboard. Most painters keep the white near the thumb-hole and go round in the order of the spectrum; yellows next, then reds, and so on, as in the list above.

Keep things orderly. There is no reason at all why a painter's materials should be in the squalid muddle that one often sees. A carpenter in his workshop knows where every tool is, and keeps them all sharp. In the same way, your tubes can be kept in order in the paintbox, or better, out on a table; put the caps back on the tubes at once after using, and squeeze only from the bottom.

You will also need turpentine, linseed oil, and turps substitute. The oil and turps make up your painting medium; a third of oil to two-thirds of turps makes a good mixture. Use turps or substitute for cleaning brushes. Don't buy little bottles; large quantities work out much cheaper.

Supports

By this word we mean anything that can be painted on; for our purposes, canvas or some form of panel. Good quality canvas can be bought ready primed and stretched, but it is expensive. On the other hand, panels worth painting on are hardly ever found in shops, and it is much better to know how to prepare your own.

Whether you use panels or canvas must be a matter of taste. Panels are cheaper, stronger, more rigid and capable of greater variety of surface, but many people like the slight feeling of 'give' and springiness that only a stretched canvas can give.

It is in making your own supports that the greatest saving of money - at the expense of time, of course - can be made. Besides, the texture of the surface you paint on is so important that everyone should know how to prepare his own. It is only by experiment that you can find the ideal surface - smooth without slipperiness, or rough without harshness.

A poor, or unsympathetic, surface can affect a picture right from the first brush stroke. The paint, instead of going on sweetly, seems to fight you all the way. Some commercially prepared panels seem to drink up the paint, so that however freely and solidly you work, the surface always appears meagre. You want to keep your paint for painting the picture - not for building up an additional priming! But sometimes the surface only becomes attractive to work on after a lot of paint has been put on to it.

Many people do not realise the paramount importance of the ground, and paint on any old thing that happens to be handy - particularly when they are learning to paint. But this is just when they need all the help they can get from their materials. To use poor supports and scruffy old brushes is rather like trying to learn cabinet-making with firewood and blunt chisels.

Let us take the preparation of canvas first. Stretchers had better be bought ready cut, unless you are a good carpenter. Unprepared (raw) canvas can be bought by the yard from department stores.

Having put the lengths of
stretcher together - make sure
that the bevelled side goes next
to the canvas - cut a piece of
canvas about 2″ wider all round
than the stretcher. Lay this
down on the floor with the
stretcher on top of it (Fig. 1).

Then proceed like this: drive
in a tack in the middle of one
side on the edge of the
stretcher. Go over to the middle
of the opposite side, pull tight
and tack (Fig. 2).

Now do the same on the
other two sides. Next, work
outwards from middles to
corners, so that you are pulling
diagonally across the canvas
each time.

When you get to the corners,
fold the canvas over neatly, and
then tack it along the back
of the stretcher (Fig. 3).

The result should be a
smoothly stretched canvas,
ready for preparation. The same
procedure would be followed if
you were stretching a ready
primed canvas.

Don't bother about the corner
wedges at this stage. They
should be hammered into the
corners of the stretcher later,
if any slack develops in the
finished canvas.

Fig. 1

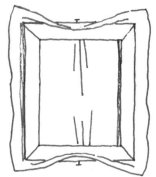

Fig. 2

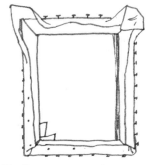

Fig. 3

Sizing

This is necessary to make the canvas less absorbent and to isolate it from the priming. The best quality is rabbit-skin size. If you can't get this, use ordinary sheet glue (cabinet-maker's glue) thinned down.

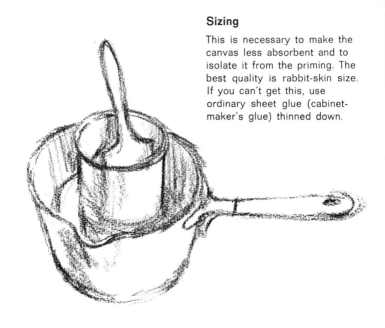

At a pinch, ordinary powdered size from a hardware or paint store can be used, but it is not likely to be of very good quality. The size must first be soaked in a little water - just enough to cover it - then hot water is poured on and the whole lot is heated up until well dissolved. Use a tin in a saucepan, as shown in the illustration.

The exact proportions are hard to give, as different sorts of size differ in strength. You could try a mixture of about 1 : 8; that is to say, one part of soaked size to eight parts of hot water. When the size cools, it should set into a soft but firm jelly. It can be heated up again, but should never be boiled, as this reduces its strength. Size left in the form of a jelly will go bad after a few days.

Put on two coats of the warm liquid size, allowing each to dry. The surface is then ready for priming.

Priming

This serves two functions. One is to produce an attractive surface to take the paint; the other is to make the support a solid pure white. All oil paint gets more transparent with age, as well as darker, and the white ground, by shining through to some extent, helps to keep the picture luminous.

Give the support two coats of a good quality white oil primer. Ordinary household undercoat can be used, but again it is rather doubtful in quality. Try to get genuine white lead undercoat. You can often buy white lead ground in oil to a stiff paste at a good builders' merchant. (This is called 'white lead in oil' in the U.S.A.) It can be thinned with turpentine and makes an excellent primer.

Panels of hardboard, wood or cardboard can be prepared in exactly the same way. If you like a rougher surface, thin canvas or linen can be stuck down on the panel with size and then primed.

Alternative primers are acrylic 'hardboard primer' and gesso. The former can be used on any surface without preliminary sizing, and as it also dries very quickly, it is by far the most convenient method; but it is much more expensive, and some painters don't like the slightly greasy feel of the surface.

Gesso is the oldest and most traditional primer, as well as the cheapest. It should not be used on canvas, however, as it is more brittle than white lead. Size the board first; then mix some powdered chalk or whitening with the liquid size until it is about the consistency of cream, and brush on while still warm. A gesso panel will probably need an extra coat of size on the top when dry, as it is more absorbent than other primers.

I have gone into this question of the preparation of canvas and panels in some detail, as I am sure it is technically one of the most important and most often neglected factors in painting.

Other media

Of course there is no reason why you should not use any medium for painting a portrait, but the oil medium has many practical advantages which make it ideal. Besides its great flexibility and range of tone and colour, alterations can be

made at any stage with comparative ease. All the water-based media - gouache, watercolour, and the new acrylic colours - dry more quickly, which makes it very difficult to move the paint about. It is almost impossible to make alterations in the transparent medium of watercolour.

Pastel, on the other hand, has many advantages. It has some of the qualities of both painting and drawing. The colour can be built up gradually, remains the same value, and can be removed and altered with ease. It is a pity that pastel has become associated with the more sugary type of children's portraits. It is a beautiful medium, and there is nothing weak or sweet in its use by great artists like Degas, Chardin or Manet.

If you want to use pastel, a good support is as essential as in oil painting. The paper should be sufficiently tough to stand up to rubbing, have enough 'tooth' to hold the pastel grains, and be an attractive colour - it is difficult to work on a dead white ground.

A grey or buff colour is pleasant to work on. It is not necessary to have a tremendous range of pastels - in fact those elaborate boxes with dozens of different tones of each colour are more of a hindrance than a help. But you will need rather more neutral colours - greys, buffs, and so on - as well as the obvious bright ones. The reason is that it is more difficult to 'mix' neutrals from the pure colours than it is in oil paint.

It is probably best to start on the basis of a drawing, perhaps in brown or sepia, which is gradually developed in colour by the use of hatchings of one pastel over another. Smudging with the finger can be useful when covering a large area, but tends to look 'sleepy'. Use it as a basis for subsequent hatching. As soon as the surface gets difficult to work into, fix it lightly. Apply the fixative with a mouth spray or atomiser; aerosol cans are a very expensive way of buying it.

Degas used to work his pastels over and over, fixing between each layer, until the surface had something of the richness of oil paint. But it is very difficult to retain the freshness which is so characteristic of this medium; it easily becomes laboured and heavy, and it is probably better to try and work quickly.

Gouache has something of the same freshness and charm of pastel, and could be used for portraits on a small scale. It can be used very like oil paint, but it has the big disadvantage that the colours dry lighter.

The studio

Besides your basic materials, you must have somewhere to work. I don't believe there is any room which cannot be made perfectly suitable to paint in. Paul Klee worked in a small kitchen, Bonnard often in a hotel bedroom. Many people think that portraits can only be painted in a studio with a high north window, but in fact such a room can be rather depressing. I like to be able to look out of the window and feel that there is some life going on around me. So I have always painted in a perfectly ordinary room and, at

present, I work in a room opening on to the garden. Things and people look natural in such a room in a way that they never can in the cold light of the traditional 'artist's studio'. In any case, hardly any artists nowadays can afford a studio like this. They are mostly occupied by rich dilettantes who use them for parties. You are much more likely to find yourself working at close quarters, as shown on this page;

Drawing a head 'sight-size

and perhaps, after all, you are more likely to produce interesting work this way. For one thing, you will be restricted to a fairly small size, probably only a head and shoulders. This is likely to give your work greater concentration and intensity. Also your model will feel more at home, surrounded by ordinary things, and you will be able to use natural backgrounds.

Neither does it do any harm to have to work close up to your sitter. It is much easier, in fact, to get measurements right if the image on your canvas corresponds in scale to the size that you see the model, as shown in the drawing. This is called working 'sight-size'. In normal art-school conditions, you may be standing fifteen feet away from the model. The actual size you see the head, if you measure it off against the edge of the canvas, may be only a couple of inches. This means every distance has to be enlarged, by an unconscious mental arithmetic, up to the scale of your picture.

Also, you can't really see a lot of the smaller forms in the head unless you are pretty close. This must depend on your own eyesight. Being short-sighted, I like to work about four to six feet away from the model.

You will need some sort of easel, wherever and however you paint. All that is necessary is that it should be rigid. The drawing shows the two most satisfactory types. The ordinary radial easel will be perfectly satisfactory for nearly all purposes. A small folding easel is really only suitable for quite small pictures.

Most painters like to have a table next to them so that all their materials are easily to hand. If you can get hold of one of those tea-trolleys on castors, you will have the ideal painting table. Instead of holding the palette, it is much easier to work with it on the table, leaving both hands free; or you may find it easier to dispense with the palette altogether, and use the table top to mix colours on.

Studio easel   Radial easel

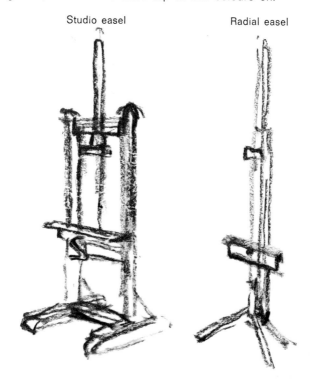

2 Drawing - the construction of the head

For our purposes, drawing can be defined as getting things the right shape, the right size, and in the right position in relation to other shapes.

It is easy to make a great mystery about drawing, and practically everyone gets an inferiority complex about it at some stage or another; 'I like painting, but I can't draw' is the gist of many remarks one hears.

I think one trouble is that many people think of drawing as meaning exclusively drawing with a lead pencil, with all its concomitant difficulties of line, modelling and so on. But a drawing can be made with any instrument that will make a mark, and one is drawing, in the sense of the definition above, all the time one is painting.

Every time a mark is made on a picture, a relationship is set up and the position of something becomes more defined.

For the purposes of painting a portrait, it is very important that these marks, which define the position of forms, should be reasonably accurate; so our first job is to try to attain some kind of precision. This means a threefold process: learning how to look, how to measure accurately, and how to make marks which will establish these measurements.

Let us go back to the person who says he can't draw a line. Ask him to draw you a map to show how to get somewhere. He will, without the slightest hesitation, start drawing a complex arrangement of lines, angles and distances. He is making a drawing.

For the map or diagram is the simplest form of drawing; and even the most sophisticated drawing still has some of its characteristics. It is still made up of lines which go in certain directions, have particular lengths, and meet other lines at certain angles.

I know that this leaves out all consideration of the third dimension and solidity. I am doing this purposely. In my experience of teaching drawing, the attempt to 'make things look round' is responsible for more bad drawing than anything else. In the effort to do this, placing and construction often get forgotten. But in a well constructed drawing, where shapes and proportions have been really studied, solidity and a feeling of mass should come of their own

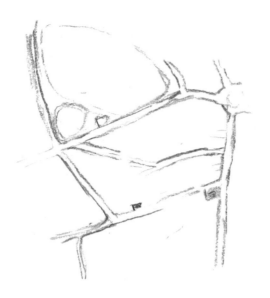

Rough drawing of a map

accord. It is as if they are the by-products of getting other things right.

The drawings here are an attempt to show those aspects· of drawing a head which are similar to drawing a map or diagram. First, distance or proportion. If one takes a measurement from eye to ear, and another from the eye to the corner of the mouth, they are seen to be in a certain ratio; in this case, very similar. This is exactly the same as estimating the length of one street in relation to another on a map.

Then, direction. The angle across the eyes, for example, slants in relation to the direction of the nose. This angle can be accurately established in just the same way as a side street can be put down on a map as running obliquely to a main road.

Drawing of a head
done in the same way

All lines can be considered as having these two qualities:
length and direction. Even curved lines can be simplified
into a series of straight tangents which run at different
angles. This is shown in the drawing on the next page.

If you get all these 'changes of direction', as we call them,
right, as well as getting the lengths of the lines right, your
drawing will turn out to be fairly accurate, considered simply as a delineation of the shapes in front of you.

It is a question of training the eye to observe these different angles. This is not quite as easy as it sounds. Nearly
everyone, when they start life drawing, under-estimates the
tilt or slope of a limb or the torso, making it go nearer to
the vertical. This gives a drawing that stiff, inflexible appearance.

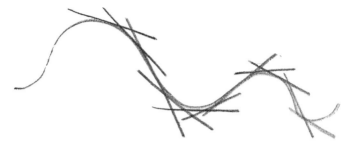

Tangents of a curve

The best way to judge an angle or direction is to hold up your pencil at the same angle and try to relate it to an actual or imaginary vertical. Try to analyse the degree of slope; say to yourself, 'This line would meet the vertical at a little less than a right-angle', or whatever it is.

There is often a vertical or horizontal line somewhere in the background which you can use as a check on other angles.

Judging angles against a vertical and a horizontal

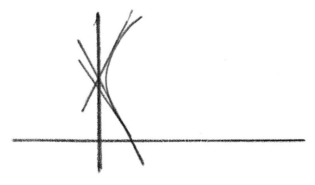

Proportion

Think of this as a question of the relative distance between various points - the distance between the eyes, for instance, in relation to the length of the nose. It is obviously easier to judge these distances if you take points that are relatively close together. As an example, it is quite difficult to judge the size of the whole head in relation to the length of the whole figure; it is easier to compare it, say, to the size of the shoulder or the distance across the chest, and to go on from there in fairly small jumps.

It's just the same with drawing a head. One of the worst ways of setting about it is to try to judge the whole shape of the head first, and then to put in the features. Many beginners do this, and find that because they have misjudged the distances, the features just won't 'fit in'.

Drawing a head

With all these points about measurement of directions and proportions in mind, let's start by making a drawing of a head in the simplest possible way. Your own face will do as well as any, with the big advantage that you can sit as long as you want to draw without worrying about whether the model will like the result or not.

Sit in front of a mirror, with a fairly simple, flat light on your face. Get as close as you like; you can then work on a fairly large scale, and you will be able to see the smaller forms more easily.

Use any medium you find congenial. There is no special virtue in using a pencil; in fact I would suggest that you use charcoal for this experiment, because it can so easily be altered by rubbing or smudging with the finger as the drawing proceeds, to modify marks that are wrong or too emphatic. It doesn't matter in the least that this process of continual alteration will probably result in an extremely messy drawing. There is no need to worry about neatness. Accuracy is quite a different matter, and that is what we are concerned with.

Sit so that your drawing is just below the object that you are looking at, and in the same line of vision - that is to say, in the case of a self-portrait, so that the board is parallel to the mirror. This is so that your eye can travel the smallest possible distance as it moves from the face to the drawing and back again.

Drawing a head from the middle outwards

In theory, you can begin a drawing anywhere. I suggest, however, that you start with a central area and work outwards. Take, for instance, the middle of the nose, between the eyes. Work across, establishing these small distances: from the side of the bridge of the nose to the pupil: across to the outside corner of the eye: across to the side of the temple. Imagine your charcoal point to be a fly walking across these small areas and pausing at each point of measurement.

The eye sockets and the eyes themselves will probably be roughly on a horizontal. Check this. Don't bother yet about the more subtle drawing of eyelids and so on. At this stage, you are concerned with making marks on the paper to establish the position of points on the form, rather than with making connected linear shapes. These will develop as the drawing goes on from a conglomeration of separate measurements.

Continue the drawing in the same way, developing outwards from your central area. Take particular care with the
length of the nose, measuring from the corner of the eye
down to the nostril. It sometimes helps to connect points
like these with a faint line, as I have done here. Keep re-
checking all these positions; don't forget all about the eyes
because you have got as far as the chin, but go back
continually to what you have already established and alter
it if necessary in the light of the new information you are
gathering. Try to see the whole thing together.

As you go on, you will find shapes and relationships that
you never knew existed, things connecting with each other,
or going parallel or opposing each other. Regard every
drawing you make as a process of discovery.

There are two points I would like to make about this first drawing. One is about vertical relationships - the position of parts of the head above or below other parts. The process known as 'plumbing' is essential. Take any point and find out which other points come directly under it; for instance, the corner of the mouth may come under the centre of the eye. You can do this most easily by holding up a pencil to make a vertical. It is very easy to go completely wrong over these measurements. Watch, in this way, the placing of the central line of the head. The drawing below shows what I mean. In a full-face drawing, it will come between the eyebrows, through the tip of the nose and the centre of the mouth. A turn of the head would change this relationship, of course. Keep this central axis firmly in mind, and try to relate the two sides of the head to it.

The other point is about making alterations. You must always be prepared to make drastic alterations, but don't get into the habit of rubbing out all the time. It is better to go on re-drawing, putting one line over or next to another. Only rub out completely when desperate!

Plumbing   Negative shapes - 'X'

Negative shapes

This is the term used to describe those areas between or behind the actual solid forms you are drawing. They are blank spaces which tend to be ignored, but which are of the greatest importance both in drawing and painting. In the drawing opposite, I have emphasised some of these shapes, in the background and round the chair, for instance. The rather blank shapes in the hair and the head are not strictly negative in this sense, as they are part of the actual form, but for our purpose here they can be used in much the same way.

The important thing about negative shapes is that one hasn't any preconceived ideas about what they are like or how to draw them. They have to be regarded as purely abstract shapes, and accordingly got right by sheer observation. One of the difficulties about drawing or painting a head is that we have all sorts of preconceptions based on years of knowledge of faces, people, and pictures.

This knowledge might be supposed to be an advantage; but in painting, as in so many other fields, preconceived ideas can prevent you from looking closely at the actual facts.

If you try to draw the negative shapes and spaces with as much care as you give to the rest of the structure, you will find it a tremendous help. They give you an additional check on proportions and directions. The tilt of an arm may not be quite right, for example; so look at the space between it and the chair. If you get that shape right, the arm will automatically be corrected.

Tone, planes and modelling

So far we have considered drawing simply as a question of measurement, of getting things into the right place. In my opinion, this is the sort of drawing that you will find of most help while you are actually painting. That is why I have given it so much importance.

But of course there is more to drawing a head than this. We are dealing with a solid structure of great complexity; it is made up of planes, large and small, flat and curved, all of which are affected by the light falling on them. This is where a lot of people get stuck.

To begin with, let's get rid of the idea of 'shading', with its suggestion of copying shadows. Think only in terms of

Fig. 1

Strong and gradual change
of planes, caused by different
lighting

Fig. 2

planes. 'Modelling' is a better word to use than 'shading', because it implies the act of shaping and constructing something solid, rather than merely copying shadows.

Every time you make some part of the head darker in tone, visualise it as a plane or series of planes which are turning away from the light. The drawings on this page show some of the ways in which the planes of the head can be affected by the light falling on them. Fig. 1 shows a very strong contrast or opposition between the light frontal plane of the face and the dark side planes. Notice how these planes, running into each other, create a connected shape defining the form of forehead and cheekbones. Fig. 2 shows a more subtle and complex relationship of planes in the same face, but seen in a comparatively gentle light.

30

A plane can meet another, or change into another, either sharply or gently. On this page are some simplified versions of different changes of plane. You can try a useful exercise along these lines by folding and bending a piece of paper and drawing it in different lights.

The first two drawings show a sharp, angular change, compared to a more gradual one. In Fig. 3 we have a more complex series of planes, one moving into the other. This is more like the sort of thing that happens all over a head.

Notice in all these examples how important is the small area where the actual change occurs. This area is practically a line in Fig. 1, a gentler gradation in Fig. 2, and a changing affair with different directions going on in it in Fig. 3.

Nothing else that happens within the planes is quite as important as this point at which they meet and change from light to dark.

It doesn't really matter how you put down this information; if the intention is clear, a smudge or a scribble will do as well as anything. Never bother too much about the way you are drawing, or whether to do the modelling with lines running this way or that; if you are thinking about that sort of thing, the chances are that you are doing a bad drawing.

Fig. 1

Fig. 2

Fig. 3

Let us see how the head is constructed out of different planes as a solid form. The simplification of the head into either an egg-like or a box-like form, met with in much old-fashioned teaching, is just too simple. Actually it has some of the characteristics of both the egg and the box. This can be seen if we draw sections round a head and think of it as sliced across at various levels (Fig. 1).

We can see then that the top of the head has a rounded shape (a). This continues downwards towards the forehead. In some people, the forehead itself is very rounded; in others, it develops strongly marked flat side planes as it approaches the eye-sockets (b). Here, the box structure begins to take over. Except in young children, there is likely to be a more angular change of plane between the front and the side of the form (c). Below the eye sockets, the planes tend to come forward in a more triangular structure to the nose and mouth (d).

But don't be satisfied with a necessarily rather theoretical explanation like this. The structure of everyone's face is different, even if we do all have features in common. So go back to your own face in the mirror; try to look at it hard with reference to the things I have been talking about, and trace the different planes with your fingers. Notice where the bones come near the surface - the sharp changes of plane are likely to occur here.

Particular features, especially the eyes and the mouth, often get drawn 'out of context'. In the natural anxiety to get a likeness, or at any rate to make the thing look human, they get emphasised at the expense of the planes around them, and end up looking like flat shapes stuck on to the surface. Try to see how these surrounding planes build up to the feature. The mouth can be thought of as the culmination of the planes around it, the eye as an oval solid fitting nicely into its socket.

In fact it is possible to draw a perfectly convincing face, even one which has a certain 'likeness', without really delineating any of the features (Fig. 2). Here, only the larger planes, forming hollows and protuberances, have been put down, but it is remarkable how the non-existent features can be, so to speak, read into this simple structure.

There are certain errors of proportion that almost everyone makes in his first drawings of heads. A very common one is to over-emphasise the scale of the features in relation to the size of the whole head. Because the features

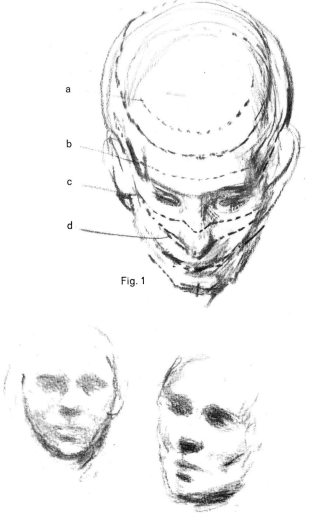

a

b

c

d

Fig. 1

Fig. 2

Fig. 3

Tessa

Notice, in the skull, the compactness of the 'features' in relation to the size of the cranium. Both the height of the cranium above the eye socket, and its width to the back of the skull, are larger than is usually realised at first. The ear, in fact, is nearer to the middle of the form than one might think.

are what we first notice about a head, and because they create the expression, we have a natural tendency to make them more 'important' in the drawing. So remember that you are not only drawing a face, but a whole head.

If you can get hold of a skull, you will notice at once that the bulk of the cranium and the back of the head is very large in proportion to the space occupied by the features. This is shown in the drawing.

Another common mistake, for some reason, is to lengthen the nose. It is generally in reality quite a compact shape, and the distance from eye to nostril is likely to be shorter than you think.

These mistakes in proportion are, of course, just as likely to occur in a painting as in a drawing. They are made by practically everybody when they start to draw portraits. At first it is very difficult to grasp the construction of the whole head, and the features are the only part of it which it seems possible to get hold of. So the bigger shapes, of which they are part, are apt to become meaningless spaces.

Nevertheless, I think it is much better to start with something that one is able to grasp, than to become too obsessed with the idea that the big forms are the only ones that matter. This is likely to lead to vague egg shapes and empty generalisations. I would prefer to start with particular, small shapes and to arrive from them at a grasp of the whole larger ones. Features and faces are, after all, what catch our eye first, and it is quite natural to want to draw them.

The drawings on this page attempt to show some of the most common failures in relationship and proportion. Fig. 1 shows the features too large for the skull. The ear, on the other hand, has become much too small and is badly placed. The ear is just as interesting as any other feature, and its position is important, coming as it does in a rather central place in the head. In this drawing there is also a lack of connection between the features as regards their position on the vertical axis of the head - the nose and mouth seem to come forward too much.

Fig. 2 shows the tendency for the shapes to become too thin and 'liney'. The eyes are too closely set, and the nose and mouth have become thin and meagre. Even narrow shapes should have a certain amplitude. Also the patches of modelling don't add up to anything - they remain quite separate.

A profile can be very attractive, besides being, in a sense, the 'easiest' way to draw a head. It implies a certain formality; the sitter is not looking anywhere near you, and is

Fig. 1

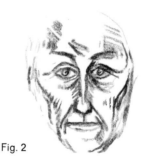

Fig. 2

hence rather detached. This is probably the reason why profile portraits are not much in favour, but many of the most beautiful portraits of the Italian Renaissance, when people didn't mind being portrayed with a degree of severity and impersonality, were pure profiles. Like a coin or a medallion, the profile is probably best treated as a flat pattern with exquisitely precise drawing and a minimum of modelling; but it can convey a very definite sense of character and likeness.

3 Composition - posing the sitter

Study for a portrait

As soon as we put anything down on the canvas - even a few brushmarks - we are beginning to compose a picture. The design of the picture is as important in a portrait as in any other subject. Because the head is the natural focus, it is a great mistake to think that it doesn't matter much what goes on in the rest of the picture. Admittedly, in the average portrait, we are dealing with a comparatively simple problem: a single figure against a reasonably plain setting. But an infinite variety is possible even within this limited framework.

In composing a portrait, the empty spaces of background round the head and figure must be considered as shapes, elements in the design as positive as the head itself, and not as mere neutral spaces. Every shape and area in a picture is important. A small area of background may not seem to matter much, but it has a part to play in holding the whole design together.

Bear in mind all the time the relation between the main shapes and the rectangle which encloses them - just as the writer of verse has to keep in mind the length and metre of the line. The shape of the area between the top of the canvas and the head, for instance, and the areas of background on either side must be satisfactory.

Of course, all this can't be considered only in linear terms. The tone and colour of these shapes alters their emphasis to such an extent that a pencil drawing done beforehand can only give an approximate idea of the effect the shapes will have on one another; still, a drawing of the kind shown on the opposite page will at any rate make one aware of them.

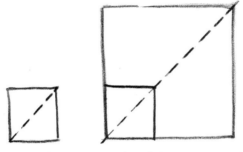

Using the diagonal to get rectangles of the same proportion

It helps to work within a rough rectangle whenever you make a drawing of this kind, rather than allowing the figure to float in a vacuum. Arrive at the rectangle by a natural process of working outwards from the figure, if possible. It should, of course, be similar in proportion to the shape of the canvas. The simplest way of arriving at this proportional relationship is by using the diagonal as shown in the drawing. In all rectangles of similar proportion, the diagonal runs at the same angle. So you can lay your drawing in the corner of the canvas and, without making any measurements, get the same proportion exactly.

Many good artists dispense with any form of preliminary drawing and prefer to design the picture directly on to the canvas. In this case, it is necessary to keep the handling as fluid and flexible as possible, and always to be prepared to make changes. The shapes, as they emerge, can then be pushed about, eased this way or that, till they begin to make sense; and even larger, more drastic changes can be made ruthlessly. Obviously, if the design is at all in an unsettled state, it is unwise to establish the smaller shapes - such as the features - too definitely; the painting must begin with the large shapes.

Soutine is a good example of a painter who never, as far as one knows, made preliminary studies. Everything he did was the result of his reactions to the model in front of the canvas. He preferred to work over old pictures, so the proportion of the canvas was settled from the beginning, and the figure was placed within this area with great instinctive sensitivity to the shapes formed by the background and clothes.

In the chapter on materials I discussed the advantages of making your own panels. Any shape and size can then be easily cut to suit the individual picture. A painter who relies on commercially prepared supports finds himself using over and over again the same sizes - 20 x 16, 20 x 24, 30 x 25 and so on. There is no particular reason why one size or shape should be better than another (apart from the chance of finding a ready-made frame to fit a stock size). One is far more likely to get into repetitive habits, using the same sort of design simply because it fits a certain size.

It is worthwhile making an effort to get away from obvious ways of designing a portrait. This can often be helped by using an unusual proportion. So try to keep a stock of panels and canvases of different shapes by you.

The design of the portrait arises from the pose of the sitter. Like every other aspect of portrait painting, it cannot be considered in the abstract, but must relate to the character of the model. Here is another of the compromises that we have to make all the time; for the pose must be one which is both natural to the sitter and typical of his temperament, and easy to hold. This is even more important

if the portrait is likely to take a number of sittings.

One always wants to get straight to work on a picture; but it is well worth exercising a little self-restraint here, and spending the first sitting in trying out some different poses. Make some small drawings; these can be very slight, like the ones on this page, merely an indication of the general lines of the pose. Even if the portrait is to be no more than a head and shoulders, experiment with some different angles, and do give your model plenty of rests. Let him or her move about the room and relax completely. A sitter who has been rather stiff or self-conscious will often, when let off the hook, unconsciously take up a much more expressive and natural pose.

This is a good argument for painting people in their own surroundings. A woman in her own kitchen, a man at his desk, are relaxed and at ease. They are, unfortunately, often also too much in charge of the situation for the concentration of the painter. He won't have them under his thumb, the telephone will ring, and he will need to exercise some cunning and patience to control the situation. But at least the sitter will look as he looks to other people. Put him on a throne in a north-lit studio, and you can see why many people equate being painted with a visit to the dentist. I think the sitter's throne, which raises him up self-consciously above his usual floor-based life, is largely responsible for this. Personally I never use a throne; but then I prefer to paint sitting down, with regular breaks to get back from the picture, and I find that the advantages outweigh the drawbacks. The sitter doesn't feel so much that something is being done to him.

But if you prefer to stand, then the sitter must be raised up nearer to your eye-level; or the head will appear sunk into the shoulders, and the far shoulder will cut against the cheek in an awkward way.

If you are painting a half-length portrait which includes the hands, make sure that your design allows for enough space round the figure. This seems an obvious statement, but many portraits of this kind do tend to become a little crowded, with the head at the top, the hands at the bottom, and large areas of clothing filling the whole central part of the canvas. Naturally the head and the hands form the most important focal points, and they look a bit uncomfortable if pushed to the top or bottom edges.

If you look at some portraits by Rembrandt, you will see how often he uses large simple areas all around the figure. This gives great stability to the design. Never be afraid of simple spaces in a portrait. Many beginners seem to think that every part of the canvas must be filled with something or else the picture will be dull and empty. But on the contrary, these comparatively 'open' spaces make a most valuable foil to the complexity of the head and figure.

The same can apply to the sitter's clothes. Rather than modelling every fold until it competes with the complex forms of the head, it is often advisable to simplify them into almost flat shapes. Almost any portrait by Modigliani will serve to illustrate this point.

'All elbows and knees'
Yet this sort of angularity can make a very interesting design

This business of composing a half-length figure was easier in Rembrandt's day, because his sitters wore longer clothes, so that the area below the hands was more unified with the rest of the picture. Nowadays we have to deal with people's knees and elbows more, and they sometimes present quite a problem. A woman sitting with her hands in her lap, in an ordinary short skirt, sometimes produces the sort of design shown in the drawing. Whatever one does, the legs seem to get awkwardly cut off by the bottom of the picture.

The short skirt, or sleeves just above the elbow, often give a feeling of angularity because the joint or articulation is emphasised; whereas a sleeveless dress will allow the whole arm to flow as a single form, and a long sleeve will emphasise the hand.

This is another reason for trying to get away from the conventional, here-I-am-being-painted pose. Have a table in the studio. Give your sitter a cup of coffee and let her talk, leaning comfortably on the table. Watch the movement of her hands and arms like a hawk. You are much more likely to arrive at a pose that is both comfortable and characteristic.

The main point to watch in the arrangement of arms and hands is that they must look natural and unforced. Unless they contribute to the design and help to show something of the personality of the sitter, it is better to reduce the scale of the picture and leave them out. They should never look as if they have been worried over.

Now let us consider the treatment of the background. The average portrait consists of three elements: head (and hands, if included), clothes, and background. Unfortunately the latter, which may well take up the largest area in the picture, is often the least considered. There are two main pitfalls here. One is to resort to a conventional formula. The dark curtains which used to hang in folds behind the sitter in practically every 'presentation portrait' are an obvious example. This has fortunately become outmoded. A more usual danger nowadays is to put down a completely unrelated area of colour, against which the head has never actually been seen or studied.

The point I want to make here is that anything which happens to be going on behind the sitter's head is likely to be more interesting, if painted with reasonable sensitivity, than a background which has been 'made up'. So try to use what is there; and if it is unsuitable, alter the actual setting rather than invent something.

The drawing on p. 43 shows a sitter in the normal surroundings of an ordinary room. The actual shapes are far more interesting than anything the painter is likely to invent.

No object that you are painting can be studied apart from its surroundings - nothing is isolated. This is true of any kind of objective painting. It applies particularly in painting a head, because the quality of the edges and the variations in colour are so subtle that to alter arbitrarily the tone or colour of the surrounding areas is likely to give an unconvincing, 'cut-out' effect. The only exception is when the painting is of a heraldic character, where realism is not sought. The background can then be considered as a colour area against which the head is placed, as on a playing card. Examples can be found in Elizabethan portrait miniatures by Nicholas Hilliard and other artists. Even here, though, it would help to study the head in relation to the colour chosen.

I would suggest, then, that you use either the normal surroundings of the room you are painting in - walls, doors and furniture - or else the simplest background possible. In both cases, paint what you see, and paint it at the same time as the head.

It is useful to have a screen which has been painted a different colour on each side. Neutral colours, such as a warm grey or a bluish grey, can produce a considerable

Different backgrounds in an ordinary room

variety of tone according to their angle to the light, and a further variation can be achieved by using two leaves of the screen at different angles. The perpendicular created by the join or the edge of the screen can be useful in dividing a large area.

If you are using the natural surroundings of a room, the problem is obviously much easier if you avoid having too much of a muddle behind the head. A bookcase or other conglomeration of small objects can look fussy and confused. But by shifting your viewpoint, even fractionally, literally hundreds of alternative compositions can be found in a single room. The drawings on p. 45 show some of the possibilities in the corner of a room.

Painters like Vuillard made most interesting designs by accepting the fact that in certain surroundings, the sitter may almost merge into a complicated background. The surroundings, instead of being kept subordinate, are painted in such a way that they almost come forward on to the same plane as the figure, and the whole picture becomes a complex network of shapes. We do often see people like this, after all, and there is no reason why backgrounds should always be regarded as totally subordinate.

In this question of composition, every piece of advice and every attempt to formulate 'rules' can be questioned. More than in most subjects, one becomes very conscious that there are exceptions to practically everything one says. So forget about all the 'rules of composition'. Instead, get into the habit of looking hard at what is around you; and if you like what you see, try to make something of it.

Never accept unquestioningly anything you may read about composition. Someone may tell you, for instance, that the face in a portrait should not 'look out of the picture', or that the background should be darker than the flesh in order that it should 'go back'. Make a habit of always asking yourself 'why?' when you come across one of these rules. Some people get so many into their heads that painting, for them, becomes almost a matter of police regulations.

Stravinsky, the composer, once said·'Academicism results when the reason for the rule changes, but not the rule'.

4 Painting a portrait

If we were living in the seventeenth century, this chapter would be a straightforward business, and a good deal easier to write. Painters then worked according to generally accepted rules and methods, and a head was built up in clearly defined stages. The end result was visualised before the painter started work; the whole process was in fact a craft.

Nowadays there are no methods; every painter has to evolve his own. The order in which he does things may change from picture to picture, according to the subject. Painting a head, or anything else, is more of a hit-and-miss process of discovery. Wilson Steer, when asked about his methods of painting, said 'Well, I muddle about until something comes'. Of course, a good painter will do his muddling about with a great deal of sensitivity and intelligence; but it remains true, I think, that most artists painting a head nowadays can't say beforehand what will happen. It is an empirical process.

So I must make it clear that I am not attempting to give you a way of painting, or any definite 'technique' for painting a portrait. All I can do is to point out some things that are likely to be useful, whatever your own way of working.

The first thing you will need is obvious - someone to sit for you. In the chapter on drawing, I recommended that for your first attempts you should sit for yourself. I think you could do worse than follow the same plan for your first attempts at painting a portrait. These are not likely to be particularly flattering likenesses - in fact that is just about the last thing you should try for at this stage. It doesn't matter whether you like your own face or not - you are simply an object to study. You will probably have a good deal of alteration and repainting to do, all of which takes time, and one of the difficulties about painting portraits is that so often one is working against time - the sitter's time. Painting yourself, you can go as slowly as you like. Remember that very few self-portraits are good likenesses, so you mustn't mind too much when you show the result to someone who says 'Who's that a portrait of?'

Setting up the mirror and easel for a self-portrait is not as simple a matter as it sounds. It is quite difficult to arrange things so that you can see what you are doing. If the face is well lit, you find that the picture is in shadow, or you can't see your palette. Try not to have the face too much lost in shadow.

A simple self-portrait is reproduced on pp. 49, 51 and 53 in three stages of development. I made the problem as simple as possible by placing the mirror on the easel and propping the small panel against it, as in the drawing below. The mirror-image then comes just above the painted one. Notice that you are seeing your face about half its actual size. Your painting can be the same scale, thus making it exactly 'sight-size'. (If you draw a line round your reflection in the mirror, you will notice a curious fact: it doesn't matter whether you are close to the mirror or at arm's length, the image remains the same size.)

One way of setting up the mirror for a self-portrait

Jane

But however you arrange the mirror, try to do it so that you don't need to move your head to see the reflection.

There are obviously hundreds of different ways of starting any picture, but we must begin somewhere. I would suggest that you first decide on the placing of the head in the rectangle. At this stage, it need be only just enough to give an idea of the size and scale.

There is not all that difference between drawing and painting, and one of the purposes of this exercise is to lead on from the drawing of your own face that we discussed earlier, to a painting considered in somewhat the same way. We are going to concentrate on the same fundamentals: getting things the right shape, and in the right place. But one of the major differences is this. When you start a drawing, the placing of the head on the paper is not a vital consideration. There is plenty of paper all around, and as long as the head is reasonably comfortable on the page, there is nothing to worry about. But in a painting, the whole shape needs to be considered in relation to the edges of the rectangle you are working in.

You will notice that in the first stage, which is more or less a drawing with the brush, I have not attempted to establish the outside shape of the head very precisely. I prefer to give myself a rough shape to work in, and then to go into the middle of it and start working outwards. So the next step is to begin placing some points within the head, exactly as we did in the drawing. In this particular case, I began with a central point: the bridge of the nose. From here I worked across to the eyes, using the shape of the spectacles. By the way, if you are painting someone who habitually wears glasses, don't try to avoid difficulties by asking him to leave them off. It is much better to use them, even if it means you can't see the eyes so completely; the shape of the frames can be very useful in giving an additional pattern of lines connecting the features.

I suggest that you use the brush right from the beginning. If you start by drawing on the panel with charcoal, you have to switch from one way of working to another. It is best to use the same tool throughout. Use a brush that is small enough to place points and lines accurately, yet is large enough to hold plenty of colour.

Use the paint fairly thin at this stage. Turps alone is all you need as a medium. I prefer to start straightaway in

Self-portrait: first stage

colour, rather than risk setting too monochromatic a key. If you start with brown or raw umber, there is a danger that it will pervade the subsequent stages and inhibit your use of colour. I started this picture with a greenish-blue colour for the first stage of drawing on to the panel. There is no break or gap between drawing and painting; patches of tone, such as the shadow down the forehead, the side of the nose and the neck, begin to develop as the drawing proceeds.

If you get too elaborate and linear a drawing on the panel, you will be tempted merely to 'fill it in' with colour. You will be too anxious not to lose the drawing, and will work in a tentative way. Don't forget: everything that you do at this stage is provisional, and drastic alterations may be necessary. When you want to alter something, wipe it out with a rag.

The second stage shows the tonal structure of the head carried further. Colour is now being used, though in a simplified way. The shadow side of the face has been put down as a rather flat area of paint, which will be worked into later; but the colour is not monochromatic, even at this stage. There is a change from warmer shadow in the middle of the head to a cooler, more greenish colour on the forehead and neck. Viridian is a useful colour for cooling these darker mixtures. As far as I remember, I used burnt sienna as well; a mixture of a warm and a cool colour like these two can be modified from neutral towards either warm or cool.

The light side of the head has hardly been touched. It is waiting while the areas around it develop in tone and colour. The background has become more complete, and the change from dark against the light side of the head to light against the dark side has been very carefully studied. I like to surround the head with these areas of tone, so that everything that happens in the head itself will be related to the background. Every patch of colour, right out to the edges of the picture, helps the others.

The larger, darker parts like the hair and the jersey have been put in as close to their final tone and colour as possible. If you work roughly from dark to light, beginning with the low-toned areas and relating the lighter ones to them, you will find it easier to keep the tone of the whole picture under control.

This is one of the most important things you have to do when painting a head. A picture which is 'jumpy' in tone - where, for example, some of the planes on the light side of the head are a little too dark - will never look right in colour. We will be going into this question of tone and colour later. For the moment, I would suggest that you try to analyse the whole set-up in terms of a simple division

Self-portrait: second stage

into light, dark and middle-toned areas. Watch the changes of tone within each area very carefully; compare, for example, a lighter patch in a predominantly dark area with a darker plane within a light area, and try to decide on their relative value. The diagram over the page will help to explain this. A dark part, the hair for instance, may have a tone in it (*a* in the diagram) which appears considerably

Tonal range from dark to light

a   b

Is a the same tone as b?

lighter. It is easy to get this too light, misled by the way it contrasts with its surroundings. In the same way, a small dark accent such as the shadow in the corner of the mouth may at first strike you as stronger than it really is.

The third photograph shows the head approaching completion. A wide range of half-tones has been added to the rather simple light-and-dark structure of the preceding stage, but the whole pattern of light and dark has not changed. In other words, these half-tones are closely related either to the darks or to the lights. Every area has been worked into with small touches, defining slight changes of plane, tone and colour. But the brush is still being used to draw with; as far as possible every brush stroke has been used to build up the construction of the shapes, as well as to alter colour and tone.

This is very important, whatever idiom you may be working in. It is fairly obvious in this particular example, where the shapes are allowed to emerge from a rather vague and flexible indication and are gradually strengthened; but it would apply even if you were working in a more linear way. Suppose you started with a complete drawing on the canvas, and then proceeded to fill in the shapes with colour. Though, as I said, this is inclined to produce a tinted drawing rather than a painting, it is nevertheless a perfectly possible method. It was the common practice in the Renaissance, and a fresco painter, for example, is almost bound to work like this.

Self portrait: third stage

But however accurate your first drawing, you would find
yourself inevitably altering the shapes as you developed
them in colour. The process of adding tone and colour to
a shape alters its character, and makes it different in all
sorts of subtle ways from the same shape as defined by
a line. X-ray photographs of Renaissance pictures often
show how the first lines of the drawing were modified as the
painting proceeded.

There has been a good deal of adjustment in the placing and drawing of the features, as other things became more defined. It is tempting to 'fix' the features too clearly at an early stage, only to find that something is in the wrong place and has to be repainted! It is therefore best to avoid accents until a much later stage.

A varying degree of emphasis is also noticeable at this point; that is, some parts of the face are seen more clearly and sharply than others. Take a contour like the line of the jaw. On the shadow side it is practically invisible, lost in the cool shadow. Indeed, in comparison with the sharp accents and clear shapes of other parts of the face, all this area is rather merged together, though the shadow is not dark. The change from light to shadow across the chin is, in fact, stronger than anything else round here. As we come round the chin, the jaw-line becomes slightly clearer. The plane under the jaw on the light side of the face is marked by a faint shadow. It is not until it joins the neck and moves up to the ear, that any sharp contour or accent is visible.

This continuous change of emphasis from 'lost' to 'found' gives a certain richness and variety to a painting. But it is not an essential quality. Many fine paintings of heads, from Botticelli to Modigliani, are bounded by a regular contour. A painter who is essentially a draughtsman and thinks in terms of line, or one who uses flat areas of strong colour like Matisse, will be justified in ignoring the way that shapes lose themselves in shadow.

The line of the cheek has been altered several times. This contour is in fact the edge of a receding plane, and if it is made too rigid, you may find that the cheek refuses to 'go round the corner'. However, this does not mean that such an edge can be blurred or evaded. You may need to scrape it down with a palette knife to loosen up the paint, so that the shape can be re-stated.

The mouth and the lower jaw are the mobile parts of the face. Their shape can alter. But the construction round the nose, eye-sockets and cheekbones is relatively static: it all moves together as one piece. I would suggest that you keep going back to this rigid structure, working from it towards the more flexible parts of the head.

As the painting proceeds, you will find yourself using the paint more solidly. This happens naturally, because you are working in smaller, more precise touches and these touches overlap to some extent; so they have to be more opaque. The thickness or thinness of the paint should be allowed to develop naturally in this way. There is no need to be too conscious of the sort of surface you are making. In general, use as little medium as possible; I use a mixture of a third of oil to two-thirds of turps in the later stages, and turps alone when starting a picture.

Highlights should not be used as an easy way to make the form look solid. It is easy to make them meretricious and exaggerated. Build the forms up towards the lightest points, and leave them till everything else is well advanced. The enlarged detail from a portrait shown here demonstrates some of the points I have been making: the building up in small touches, the changes in emphasis and accent, the discreet use of highlights, and the variety of surface obtained by using the paint solidly.

5 Colour and tone (value)

A natural colour sense is quite a rare thing. Most painters develop their sensitivity to colour gradually. In fact, some of the greatest colourists - Van Gogh, Cézanne, Monet - began by painting low-toned pictures, using a lot of black. So don't worry too much if your first attempts at painting a head are dull in colour. It is much better than to attempt flashy 'effects'.

We all have a liking for clear bright colours, but low-keyed colour can be equally beautiful. Concentrate on keeping the colour clean and getting the relationships right. It should always be decisive, even if it is only a matter of khakis and greys. It should be mixed on the palette, and not on the picture.

The variety of subtle changes of colour found in flesh can be simplified into a general distinction between 'warm' and 'cool' colours. This is particularly important when dealing with rather subtle mixtures and neutrals. A grey, for instance, can mean anything from a very cold blue-grey to a warm violet-grey, or a more neutral greenish hue. And it can look warmer or cooler according to the way it is set against other colours.

To find out something about the way that colours behave, and to discover the enormous variety of neutrals which can be made from the pure colours on your palette, it is worth spending a little time doing some simple exercises in colour mixing and colour juxtaposition. Here are two. The first one relates to the way a grey can be affected by other colours near it.

Paint several squares of neutral grey, taking great care to get each square exactly the same colour. Then surround each square with a different pure colour, as in the diagram on the opposite page. You will find that each grey square now appears slightly different in hue.

You can continue the experiment with a bigger range of pure colour, and you can try using different amounts; that is, varying the size of the coloured square in relation to the grey. You will find that below a certain size, the pure colour ceases to have much effect on the grey.

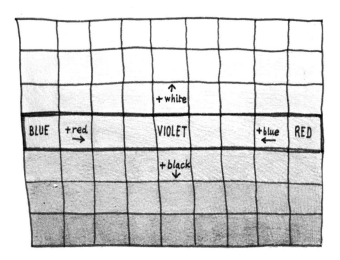

An experiment in colour mixing is shown on this page. Take two opposed colours, say a blue and a red. Paint a square of pure red at one end of the 'scale' and of blue at the other. In the middle place an equal mixture of the two (violet). Gradate the other squares evenly towards the violet with varying proportions of red and blue, so that you have a scale going in even steps from blue to blue-violet, violet, red-violet and red. Then take each mixture and make another scale going vertically, mixing each colour with white. Finally go downwards from each square, mixing with increasing amounts of black.

To have any point, this exercise should be done with precision. Each square should be painted carefully, and the colour mixed thoroughly on the palette and put down smooth and opaque. Use a white ground; a piece of ordinary white card will do perfectly. Try to make each square darker or lighter than its neighbour in a steady progression, with no 'jumps'. You can also do a similar series of squares mixing with other colours instead of black.

Colour exercises of this kind may seem rather abstract and without much connection with portrait painting. But they have a very important function: they make one more aware of the great importance of making precise mixtures on the palette, rather than approximate and accidental ones on the surface of the picture. Oil paint can be an intractable medium. In other media, such as watercolour or pastel, there is an easy, natural charm about even an accidental blob or smudge. Oil paint doesn't give you much help in this way. What charm or richness you get out of it, has to be done by you. It can be the most beautiful stuff: or it can turn into horrible greasy mud.

This can happen when the painter finds that a certain patch of colour is wrong, and proceeds to dab other colours into it to modify it; and particularly so when darker colours are painted into lighter ones. If you have put down something that is too light, scrape it out before repainting. The dark touches (unless placed very solidly as accents, which is quite a different thing)· will always be muddied by the light paint underneath. On the other hand, it is possible to paint light into dark, because the light paint, being thicker and more opaque, doesn't mix so much with what is under it.

Of course, a good painter can do almost anything with oil paint: he can push it around, churn it up, and it will still look lovely. But a beginner should try to keep the mixtures clean and to remember that bad colour is usually indecisive colour.

Another point which will emerge in our colour exercise is that black can produce beautiful mixtures. Many people will tell you that you should never use black. But of course it is a question of how you use it. I would suggest that you only make definite mixtures with it, and never paint it into existing colour. This is bound to produce a grubby and dirty quality.

Here is our last experiment, which is a little nearer to the immediate problem of painting a head. Try to analyse in

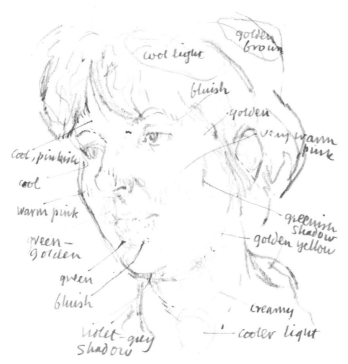

Colour notes

words the different areas of colour in a face. Make a rough drawing of your sitter, and write down as many different changes of colour as you can see. The effort to describe colour in words often forces one to look just that extra bit harder. Note with special care the difference between warm and cool areas. Try to decide if the half-tones are cooler than the lights, and what the colour is doing in the shadows.

You may, of course, feel that you can't really see any of this subtle colour that I have been talking about in the shadows! If so, don't worry. If you really think a colour is grey, or brown, put it down like that. But having done so, have another hard look at the model and compare the colour -

you may have second thoughts. Never force the colour in an objective painting. Nothing is more unpleasant than purple or green shadows in a head, put down only because the painter felt they ought to have been there.

Tone (value)

Tone (value) is so much bound up with colour that it is difficult to separate the two. As I said earlier, false tone will always make the colour look wrong. So if you feel that a piece of colour isn't working, take another look and try to find out if it is wrong tonally.

It is obvious that planes in the head which are roughly parallel and thus tilted away from the light at the same angle, will be similar in tone. This assumes that reflected light does not alter their value. It is often useful to take several such parallel planes and try to relate them to each other. You should try to achieve a continuity of tone through the head, so that the planes connect logically.

The tone of the picture is dictated by two factors: the lightness or darkness of areas - light flesh, dark clothes, and so on - and the change of tone from light to dark within an area, caused by light falling on the forms. This distinction is made clear in the drawings opposite.

Most portraits contain both kinds of tone. But remember that a picture can be tonally very satisfying by the simple juxtaposition of flat areas, with hardly any modelling. If you are using very strong colour, it is usually best to keep the areas fairly flat. Bright colour which is also heavily modelled from light to dark tends to look stodgy and overloaded. If you want big contrasts of light and shade, it is better to keep the colour relatively simple. We can see how this principle works by contrasting two kinds of picture: a Rembrandt or a Caravaggio, in which the forms are strongly modelled and the colour is almost monochromatic; and a Persian miniature or a Matisse, where simple areas of un-modulated bright colour are placed side by side.

At first you will find that there is a temptation to over-model the head - to exaggerate the difference between light and dark. This comes about in the effort to create a feeling of solidity. To make matters worse, this over-modelling can extend to other parts of the picture, so that everything becomes equally gradated from light to dark. It is worth remembering that a dark surface will not have the

Drawings after Rembrandt and Matisse

same range of tone as a light one under the same lighting conditions; thus, the contrast of light and dark will be greater on a face than on a dark sleeve.

Let us express this diagrammatically. If you think of the range of tone possible in your painting as like a piano keyboard running from dark to light, and select the 'compass' of tone on the face, it might run from c to d on the diagram. On the sitter's dark suit, though, it might cover the scale only from a to b. It is quite possible, in fact, that no part of the face is as dark as the lightest part of the suit.

You can see this 'grouping' of tones at work in the

a   b   c   d

portrait reproduced in colour facing p. 48, where a certain simplicity and breadth was aimed at.

I have gone into this question at some length because it is so often ignored, to the detriment of the unity of the picture and the quality of the colour. In painting a head we have to be continually going from the particular to the general, and back again - looking hard at one piece, and then trying to see the thing as a whole. In your self-portrait exercise you may have found yourself getting too involved with small areas. This is quite natural, and is probably to be preferred to over-generalisation. But the parts must be related to the whole.

6 Handling paint

You can do practically anything with oil paint. It is such a flexible medium that it is impossible to lay down laws for its management, apart from a few purely technical points relating to permanence. Let us deal with these first.

Even when you are painting bad pictures, it is worth assuming that they are meant to last. The attitude of 'oh well, I'm not painting for posterity' is frankly a silly one. Who knows - you may paint a picture that someone likes, and whether posterity comes into it or not, they are not going to be very pleased if it deteriorates in a year or so. It is not generally realised that nasty things can happen to an oil painting in a relatively short time. Bad priming can crack, and so can wrongly applied layers of paint. One colour may 'strike through' another, and of course certain colours may darken appreciably.

But apart from this, you are likely to paint better pictures if you are using reasonable materials in a proper way. There are, in fact, only a few simple principles to remember; it is not necessary to get like the man who reads a medical dictionary and decides he has got every disease in the book.

The first thing to remember is that oil paint has to dry in layers, unless you are able to finish the painting in one sitting. The man painting his front door has an exactly similar situation. He always works 'from lean to fat'; his first layer is an undercoat with little oil content, and after that is dry he puts on a top coat which contains more oil. If you build up your picture in the same order - first layers thin, subsequent layers thicker and fuller - you should have no trouble. The most usual cause of cracking is putting a layer of thin dark paint over thick, half-dry colour.

The second principle is that oil paint gets slightly more translucent and thinner as it ages. If you took a panel painted with black and white squares, and covered it with a thick layer of white paint, you would find that after a few years the squares were beginning to appear through the white layer. So be careful what you paint over. An old picture may be very convenient, but it will be all the better for a coat of white primer.

There is not really much else to bother about. If you use the colours suggested in the first chapter, and consult the manufacturers' lists of permanent and semi-permanent colours for the additions you will want to make, you should have no trouble with the actual paint. Don't use too much oil. There is plenty already in the colour. In the later stages, when you are working in smaller touches rather than in large areas, you can dispense with any medium, as far as possible. In the earlier stages it is only necessary to use a little turps.

As for handling the paint on the picture, the best advice one can give is to try and keep it as fresh as possible. Don't go on tinkering with the paint in a tentative way. Try to put it down in definite touches and leave it like that.

However, you will often need to lose a shape that has become too rigid or dull, in order to come back to it and re-draw. You can do this 'losing' by scraping down, or by working across the paint. An example of the latter process is shown in the details reproduced here.

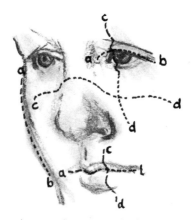

It often helps to place touches across the form, rather than along it. The diagram shows this distinction. The lines *ab* run along the shape of eye and cheek, while *cd* refers to the change of plane across them.

Fig. 1 shows part of a painting which has become too rigid and monotonous in handling. Though there is nothing much wrong with the proportion and placing, the nose has been treated too much as an 'up-and-down' shape, and the mouth as a strip going across. One can forget that the nose is built up of planes which move across the middle of the face, and is not a sort of linear strip without variety of form. The bridge of the nose actually varies in width and sharpness all the way down.

In Fig. 2 I have worked across this too linear form. This has had the effect not only of breaking up and softening the shape, but also of creating a more subtle build-up of half-tones on either side of the nose. The same thing has been done to the mouth.

Fig. 3 shows the repainting on the basis of this vague shape. The tip of the nose has been made more solid in drawing, and not so much a mere continuation of the bridge. The whole form is now built up more by considering the planes across it, and not only those running along it. Small dark touches, rather than continuous lines, accent the shape of the mouth.

Fig. 1

Fig. 2

Fig. 3

Fig. 1

Fig. 2

Now I should like to take the case history of a particular portrait, which is reproduced in colour facing p. 80. The self portrait, which we went into in some detail earlier in this book, was in the nature of an exercise, and was built up in fairly methodical stages. But many painters are unable or unwilling to follow such a precise method, particularly nowadays, and I thought it might be interesting to take a portrait, painted without any thought of demonstrating a process, through all its vicissitudes.

I must stress once again that I should be very sorry if anything in this book was to be taken as 'laying down the law'. Every painter must find out for himself the way of working that suits him. As an instance, I personally like to work rather freely, but many people have a natural leaning towards sharp precise forms and detail. If this is what interests you, I am convinced that you should paint whole-heartedly in this way and set yourself to explore ways of handling paint that allow you to give full rein to your particular leaning. I don't believe there is any virtue in painting freely or precisely, with tone or with colour, in this way or in that way; all that matters is that the result should come from your own direct observation and feeling for some particular aspect of reality, and not from an idea that it is 'right' to use this or that formula.

Many people get the idea, for example, that they should ignore all detail. But a visit to the National Gallery will show at once that some of the greatest masterpieces are full of meticulously painted detail. Admittedly, these painters were masters of their craft; but there is something to be said for the view that even a bad painter's work is more likely to be worth looking at if he errs on the side of minute particularisation than of generalisation.

But however one paints, it is likely to be a help to have a theme in mind for each picture, to give it an impetus. In a portrait, this theme need not necessarily be connected with the sitter's likeness. In this case, I wanted to use the arms and hands in the design, making a pattern surrounding the head. I had often seen the sitter in this kind of pose, and I liked the way that the light in this particular room - a kitchen - made the head and arms rather luminous and glowing in contrast to the muted greys and browns of the dress.

I made a number of rough drawings for a portrait of this sitter, some of which are shown here. At first I tried a different dress and put the sitter into various chairs and poses,

Opposite: Two stages in beginning a portrait

Studies for portrait

but eventually I returned, as often happens, to the first impression.

The painting was started on a white board which had a dull ochre colour rubbed over it. Not an ideal colour to work on, in this case; I would have preferred a cooler ground, but it was the only board I had at the time which was a suitable shape. The first tentative marks indicating the design are shown in the first colour reproduction. Notice that already colour is being used to some extent.

A simple opposition has already been set up between warm and cool colour. Notice how patches of colour are being 'tried out' on various parts of the picture; there are touches of the cool light grey behind the head, and hints of warm colour on the arm and nose. On the other hand, the dark shape of the dress has been 'rubbed in' to make a comparatively connected shape.

This is characteristic, for me, of the opening stages of a picture, before the panel is covered. Darker areas of colour are thinly scrubbed on, creating a surface that will be painted into later; other, lighter colours are indicated merely by a few disconnected touches placed next to other colours. This process serves two purposes: it establishes the darks quickly, and keeps them thin in quality; and it prevents the light areas from becoming too congested with paint. It is in the lighter parts that the most subtle changes occur, and they had better be left till later when they can be related to the whole thing. If the lights get covered too quickly, there is a danger that the tone will get too light. It is always easier to bring a tone up than to push it down: a half-tone can be turned into a light with a few touches, but a part which has become too light has to be scraped down and repainted.

This 'rubbing-in' of darker colour is best done with thin paint and a fairly stiff brush, quite freely and rapidly. The edges will be varied and irregular, but because the paint is thin it will be easy to draw into them.

The pose and the placing within the squarish shape of the panel are already established, and will remain throughout the progress of the picture; but every one of these shapes will be moved and altered, perhaps only fractionally, again and again.

The second colour reproduction (Fig. 2) shows the painting at the end of the first sitting - an hour or so after the first stage. The panel is now covered fairly completely, and the head is beginning to take shape. The features are still only indicated, however, and far more attention has been given to building up the planes of the head to show the way that the light frontal plane of the face joins the shadow area of the side of the cheek and the side of the nose. I like to establish this rather subtle change of plane, with its varying gradations, fairly early, so that it remains fresh and does not have to be continually re-stated.

The hair, too, has been treated as a single mass turning from light to dark. This change of plane in the hair must be related to that of the head as a whole; it is all part of the same form. This can be seen in the drawing below, where this change from dark to light has been purposely exaggerated.

The hair should always be painted at the same time as the face and not 'left till later'. One reason is that the edge, as it comes against the face, is very varying. In the places where it grows out from the skin, it will make a soft, gradual change, and in other places, like a fringe, it may make quite a sharp, hard edge. If it is equally defined all round, it may look like a wig!

The general colour of the picture is now more complete, and the areas of wall, cupboard and table have been stated more fully. At this stage certain dissatisfactions may become crystallised. After the sitter has gone, it is a good thing to spend some time relaxing, looking at your picture and criticising it to yourself. Try to see it freshly - put it in a different light, or look at it in a mirror. I often turn the painting upside down; this forces one to see it in another way - as an abstract.

Detail of head

Looking at this picture after the first sitting, I was fairly happy about the way the head was going, but the colour didn't look right to me. The orange-red of the wall, particularly, did not seem to have much to do with anything else. I decided to play around with this in the next sitting, and also to see if something more interesting could be made of the bin, which came somewhat awkwardly against the head.

This was, in fact, moved in the next sitting, but most of the time was spent in working on the head and the hand. This part of the picture was brought on quite a long way, as can be seen from the detail of the head on p. 69.

Another thing that had been worrying me slightly all the time was the arm resting on the table. Unconsciously, in fact, I had avoided working on it - realising, I suppose, that it was going to need some alteration. An accidental change of pose during a rest gave me the incentive to change it. It now looked more comfortable and natural, and cut out an awkward straight line.

The last sitting was spent largely on the arms and background. This was changed a good deal, though the general tone did not alter much. I don't like having to repaint background areas, as it can easily make the head appear 'cut out', and in fact the hair and the shoulder which comes against the new paint had to be repainted together with it.

No doubt I would not have needed to make these alterations if I had given the composition more thought at an early stage. But it is not always possible to plan ahead more than a certain extent. There were many other changes, some of which were so small that they will probably not be noticeable in the reproduction. The portrait is shown in colour opposite p. 80.

Perhaps this is a good place to sum up some of the most common faults in painting portraits.

1. *Exaggeration of tone or colour* In the first case this is likely to happen through a fear of 'flatness'. Tones become jumpy through lights and darks becoming too far apart and a corresponding weakness in the half-tones. Colour becomes forced usually in the direction of excessive warmth, making the face look as if covered with theatrical make-up. The relation between cool and warm is either minimised or over-emphasised.

2. *Poor, muddy colour in the flesh* This often happens through excessive repainting into wet colour, especially in the darks. The shadow areas become sooty or muddy. This may be made worse by unsatisfactory tonal relations.

3. *Stodginess* This, again, is often the result of overworking and laboriously repainting separate features. Lively, direct drawing with the brush is smoothed out and replaced by that unpleasant quality known as 'licked'.

4. *Lack of relation between features and head* Again this may be caused by over-elaboration of separate features, in a desperate endeavour to get a likeness.

Head of a girl

There is no better way of getting over difficulties like these than by regularly painting small heads in one sitting, like the one reproduced here. The speed with which you have to work forces you to keep everything going together, and also helps to keep your tone and colour simple and broad. Rapidity of execution should not mean ill-considered or hasty sketching. Try to work deliberately. The discipline of making one touch do the work of many, and of making your decisions once and for all, is very useful.

7 Getting a likeness: developing a style

There is nothing to be ashamed of in wanting to get a good likeness. It is, in some ways, the point of doing the portrait. The reason why you wanted to paint one person rather than another was because you were interested in that individual's face, and wanted to describe it. We have had to talk up to now as if likeness didn't matter at all; but this is merely to get things into the right order.

The likeness should always grow naturally out of the process of getting other things right. It should be, in a sense, a by-product rather than your first aim. You are likely to get a much more satisfying likeness in this way, because it will have a basis in solid structure.

There is nothing more dangerous to a portrait than a likeness which arrives too early. The painter then spends the rest of his time trying to hang on to it - but everything he does seems to take something away from it, and the portrait ends up neither a good painting nor a satisfactory likeness.

What is a likeness, anyway? The ideas of the sitter, the sitter's family and the painter are likely to be at some variance. Many people don't look like themselves when they are sitting rather self-consciously for a portrait. This is especially true of talkative and cheerful people; their friends think of them like that - they aren't used to seeing them sitting still.

You have to get to know your sitter, and some people take longer than others to become at their ease. Vuillard said that at the beginning of a portrait, when he didn't know the sitter well, everything went smoothly and the likeness came easily. But after a few sittings he had got to know the sitter, and the portrait no longer had any resemblance.

Watch your sitter when he is relaxed and off guard. Try to see his characteristic ways of sitting, for the likeness may come out in the angle of his head or the way he clasps his hands. This is shown very well in the portrait by Kyffin Williams reproduced on the next page. The whole figure, not only the face, is characteristic of the sitter. One can often recognise friends in the street long before their faces are visible, simply by their way of walking or the silhouette that they make. It would be an amusing exercise to paint a

Jack Jones by Kyffin Williams

73

portrait of someone seen from the back. Probably it would turn out to be much easier to get a likeness.

In dealing with the likeness of the face itself, it is often the mouth which gives trouble. You will get quite used to hearing that phrase, so familiar to portrait painters, 'It's very nice, but I think there's something not quite right about the mouth'. (Sargent's terse definition of a portrait was 'a painting with a little something wrong about the mouth'.) It is such a flexible and changing feature, and a change of a millimetre or two can completely alter the expression of a head. For this reason, take great care to build the planes round the mouth which lead up to it, before making too definite a statement about the lips themselves. Don't delineate the edge of the lips too harshly. It is a delicate and subtle contour, and there may not be very much difference of tone or colour between the lip and the flesh around it. The line between the lips, in fact, is likely to be the strongest accent in the mouth. Renoir and Manet often left the lips very under-stated, as an exquisite smudge.

If you have difficulty with likenesses, try to keep the features a little undefined in this way, and concentrate on stating with the utmost precision the proportion and shape of the head. In the later stages, those small forms which add so much to the expression - the corner of the mouth, the eyelids and so on - can be gradually defined.

One nineteenth-century painter - I think it was Hoppner - had a good method. He would show the portrait, as it progressed, to the sitter's family and friends. As soon as one of them said 'That's beginning to look like her', he knew that it was nearly time to stop.

About the worst way of painting is to spend sitting after sitting fiddling with the separate features. They get over-defined, stodgy, and out of relation to the whole head. Ideally, one should repaint the whole head if something goes wrong. It is not always possible to do this, but one of the differences between the experienced painter and the beginner is that the former is always more prepared to make drastic changes - if necessary losing everything he has built up, including nice bits of painting, in order to start afresh. Manet used to take the whole head out with petrol and a rag, right down to the bare canvas.

This happened thirty times in one particular portrait. He would repaint the whole head each time in one sitting. It must have been alarming for the model, and he couldn't have worked in this way with an impatient or unsympathetic sitter. It is a good example of the co-operation between artist and sitter which is necessary for the success of any portrait.

All the portraits reproduced in this chapter have, I think, this quality in common; all the heads look as if they were painted 'in one piece' without any fiddling about with separate features. You get the feeling that each is an excellent likeness, even without knowing the sitters, because each head has such an individual character.

And yet probably none of these painters was thinking consciously of portraying the 'character' of his model. I don't think it often happens that a painter has a strong idea, when he starts a portrait, about aspects of the sitter's personality that he wants to emphasise. In fact, it would probably not turn out so well if he had too much of a preconceived idea.

Most portraits go through many stages of 'likeness'. The sitter may look like fifty different people, one after another, in the course of a morning's work. One brush-stroke can completely alter the look of a head. What happens is that the painter, at one stage, says to himself: 'Yes, that's beginning to look right'.

This is the first period in the history of painting in which there is no generally accepted style of painting a portrait - or rather, there are hundreds of different possible ways. Before, there was always a 'period style' to which practically every artist conformed. Nowadays we are overwhelmed with reproductions of the art of all periods and images of the human face treated in every imaginable manner. There is, perhaps, no other subject that has been tackled in so many diverse ways.

We accept all these various images as convincing and valid; but someone from a completely different environment or period in which there was one recognised way of treating a head, would certainly find many of them almost unintelligible.

Take the reproductions in the average daily paper, for example. On one page there may be a photograph which we are able to recognise instantly as a well-known person; but on analysis it may be made up only of a few greyish smudges of irregular shape. Photographs, which we think of as being 'real', can in fact be extremely stylised. Another page may carry an advertising photograph cut in such a way that only the side of a face, nose and mouth are visible; the contrast of tone may make the whole of the eye disappear, and yet we can 'read' a whole face into it and recognise it as a pretty girl.

The comic strips will show a bewildering variety of stylisation - from the man with a long nose at right angles to his face and a circle for an eye, to the 'realistic' drawing which uses completely formalised hatching to represent shadows.

These drawings and paintings of heads done in various modern idioms often represent a 'conceptual' approach to the problem of representing a human being; in other words,

Painting by a child aged 9

Jane by Peter Greenham

they are not based so much on observation and analysis as
on an idea, a concept. Children's drawings are largely conceptual in character - at least, up to the age of about
twelve. The marks on this child's painting (on p. 76) stand
for eyes, nose, and mouth, though even here there is
some evidence of direct observation.

The conceptual approach is a very important one, responsible for some of the greatest works of art; but here we are dealing essentially with realistic, objective painting from the model. But even in this comparatively limited field, the variety of possible styles is bewildering.

In a period such as this, perhaps the only way to develop your own mode of expression is simply to ignore the whole question of style. I would advise you not to worry at all about which manner to adopt; look hard at your subject instead, and try to put down, in the simplest and most direct way, what you think is important about it. This may sound simple, but actually it is quite difficult to rid your mind of preconceived ideas as to what a picture ought to look like.

Don't be afraid that the result will look 'old-fashioned' or uninteresting. If your search for the true facts and relationships in your subject is done with enough intensity, something personal and interesting will emerge. And in any case, it is better to produce a halting but genuine attempt to realise something you have seen for yourself, than a flashy formula.

Kyffin Williams' portrait on p. 73 shows a personal style which has evolved gradually. Though an instantly recognisable style, it has not in any way been imposed on the sitter. It is simply the most direct way of expressing the painter's interest in his subject.

The planes of the head are built up in big, simple slabs of colour. These solid touches are put down frankly, and left without any attempt at further modulation. The other areas are kept extremely simple, and this gives full value to the rather original placing of the figure in the rectangle of the canvas. This simple, direct method has been evolved as a consequence of the artist's preference for working very quickly - his portraits are done in one sitting.

The portrait by Peter Greenham on p. 77 shows a very different way of handling paint. Here the brushwork is extremely free and loose, and the form is built up from innumerable small touches. Notice how the features are suggested, rather than delineated, in terms of tonal patches and accents. One of the fascinating things about painting is the way in which a few apparently random blotches and scrawls can construct a mouth or suggest the eye in its socket as fully as this. This portrait was painted by artificial light.

Miss Briggs by Richard Lee

This sometimes has the effect of making cast shadows, such as the one under the nose, sharper in emphasis than the form which is responsible for them, and generally simplifying and intensifying the tonal contrasts. As is natural when the modelling is strong, the colour was kept simple.

Jesus Pardo by Josef Herman

Diana

The portrait by Richard Lee on p. 79 is a good example of rather austere, deliberate drawing and construction. The forms within the head are simplified into angular straight lines, and these directions are carefully related to one another. Notice how parallel directions - such as the forehead, the nose and the ear, or the eyebrow and the mouth - are emphasised. There is,. however, no feeling of rigidity or pedantry; the cool, measured approach is kept lively by the free, rather 'open' quality of the handling.

Josef Herman's portrait (p. 80) shows a slightly different approach. It uses more abrupt and definite distortions and simplifications of the form to convey the painter's ideas about the character of his sitter. It could be described as more expressionist in character. However, Herman is using traditional methods - simplicity of tone and colour, rich and full paint quality - rather than the free and broken handling usually considered typical of expressionist painting.

But labels of this sort are very loose in their application. In fact all these painters are to some extent modifying, emphasising and simplifying the form in the interests of two things: the consistency of the painting and the character of the sitter. There is no absolute standard of 'realism'. If something strikes you as important, you are likely to stress it in your painting.

The influence of photography

Our standard of realism nowadays is likely to be the photograph. But, as I commented before, a photograph can be a highly stylised and 'unreal' image. The camera has had a long and chequered relationship with portrait painting, of course, and it has not necessarily always had a bad influence. Degas, Ingres and Sickert all used photographs. The work of the great nineteenth-century photographer Muybridge on the human figure and animals in movement has been studied and used by many painters - notably in recent years by Francis Bacon.

But on the whole, the camera has been an important element in the decline of portrait painting over the last hundred years. Everyone knows the sort of society or boardroom portrait that is obviously based on a photographic image. However much these productions try to conceal their parentage by flashy brushwork, they betray their mechanical origin by a superficial and wooden quality. They prove that likeness on its own is not enough, and that it is almost impossible to create a convincing formal structure with only a two-dimensional image to work from. The painter needs solid, living form in front of him. He may work at one remove, using drawings made from life to paint from, but that is another matter. Many fine portraits have, in fact, been painted from drawings - those of Holbein, for instance.

The good painters who have used photographs have never merely copied them. They have used them as an additional source of information - additional, that is, to study of the form carried out directly from the model, whether by drawing or painting; or else, as in Sickert's late works, they have had such long experience in direct painting that they are able to invent freely on the information that the photograph gives them.

So unless you are very experienced, don't be tempted to work from photographs. I know it is a temptation, when you have a difficult sitter who will not give up the time; and probaby every portrait painter has used them at one time or another when in dire straits. But the result will be almost bound to look hard and lifeless.

Painting from drawings

I have mentioned that many fine portraits have been carried out from drawings. This method doesn't suit everyone, but it has certain advantages. If you make a good working drawing, you can continue with the picture when the sitter isn't there. Quite often the most useful work is done on a portrait after the sitter has left. There is time to think about the progress of the picture a little more calmly, and the memory may hold on to the more important aspects of the subject. A drawing will assist this.

Then there is the type of portrait which is not entirely naturalistic, but depends to some extent on an abstraction from the actual form. This is probably better done from drawings. A working drawing can be considered simply as a way of packing in as much information as possible. Written notes about colour and tone are essential. Many painters who work from drawing develop their own kind of shorthand notation, which may be almost unintelligible to anyone else. It may be necessary to make several such studies during the course of the picture.

8 Painting children, double portraits and groups

Besides being attractive to paint in themselves, children are likely to be the subject of your first commissions. There are one or two points worth considering here, though again I would stress that for children's portraits, as for all others, there is no question of special methods - just good painting!

The most obvious difficulty about painting young children is, of course, the practical one of how to keep them still. Above the age of, say, eight or ten, it is quite possible to get real co-operation from a child. Little girls are often quite admirable sitters. Even so, their patience should never be strained; no child can be expected to sit still for long periods, and you must be prepared to work in fairly short spells. In the case of very young children, these short bursts may last only a few minutes at a time. You need a great deal of patience, and the ability to wait and watch. An expression or a tilt of the head may recur only for a few seconds at a time, and to some extent you will need to work from memory.

This use of memory is a very valuable talent for any painter, and it can be developed. We get accustomed, in any objective painting, to having our subject under our eye, so to speak, the whole time; yet the memory is being used to some extent even here. As the little girl said about her drawing, 'I look, and then I put a line round my look'. In the short space of time between looking at a model and putting a mark down on the canvas, the memory is at work. It is a question of extending this process. There are various ways of training your memory. Drawing animals in movement at a zoo is a valuable exercise. Another way is to study faces in a bus or train (don't stare too obviously) and to try to set down essential characteristics afterwards in a drawing from memory.

Some painters are able to keep their sitters entertained with lively conversation. I find this is more possible with adults than with children, and I prefer to have someone else there the whole time to read or talk to them. Sometimes the television will keep a lively child quite still for comparatively long periods, if you can concentrate on painting with Yogi Bear going on just behind you!

This little girl was a fairly lively sitter. I painted four or

Clarissa

five small heads of her, each being completed in one sitting
of about an hour and a half after tea. This is the first one -
the best painting, but the worst likeness! The advantage of
this method is that the painting never gets overworked,
and at the end you have several versions to choose from.
But it takes a good deal of experience before you can work
as fast as this.

In some ways babies are less of a problem than the four year old. They can be immobilised quite satisfactorily in a high chair, and will often get absorbed for short periods in playing with toys or just staring at you. The three to eight year old stage is the most difficult for the painter, and it is just the age when many parents want their children painted.

A child's face is comparatively unformed. It has not yet settled down into a set range of expressions, and is so mobile that the painter sometimes feels that his sitter has not just one face, but about twenty, and is able to switch from one to another with alarming rapidity. For this reason, you must try to keep the picture in a state in which it is easy to make alterations. It is better to err on the side of sketchiness and lack of definition, than to resolve the forms too rigidly and sharply - this will almost certainly give rise to the remark, 'You've made her look so much older'. If you look at a painting of a child by Renoir, you will see what I mean; often the only emphasis in the face is given to the eyes, and the other features are no more than a suggestion.

The skin is such a delicate and fresh colour in most children, and the changes of colour are so subtle, that I would suggest you use a rather flat light without much shadow or modelling. Most people think of a child's face as essentially a light shape, even more than an adult's. Be particularly careful not to 'stretch' the tones; that is, not to exaggerate the darks and lights at the expense of the half-tones.

Personally, I prefer to paint children in their own homes. They are usually more comfortable surrounded by their own atmosphere, and as I like to paint them on a small scale there is no particular trouble about working in someone else's room. In fact, I usually sit with the paint box on my knee and the panel in the lid, doing away with any necessity for an easel.

Some of the most charming portraits of the past are of two or more figures grouped together; think of Gainsborough's daughters, or Renoir's Mme. Charpentier and her children. There is a long tradition of the family portrait, especially in eighteenth-century England, when every minor portrait painter seemed capable of putting a number of figures together - all looking at the painter and all in their best clothes - without any trouble at all. We no longer have this tradition, and for us it is a tremendous test of our ability to organise a picture.

Barbara and Jane Conrad

You must try to get your sitters together for some of the time, though it is not necessary or possible to paint the whole picture with them all posing at once! The small picture reproduced here was started with the two girls sitting together; then, after the first session, I worked at them separately, usually having a short sitting from each in the course of one visit.

On the following page are studies for a larger and more ambitious family portrait - a whole group in the open air. This had to be done almost entirely from studies. I made innumerable drawings and small oil studies like these, and a larger and fairly elaborate study for the landscape. These were all done on the spot over quite a long period, during which the foliage of the trees changed considerably!

The picture itself was painted completely indoors, and fairly quickly compared with the long period spent in making studies. After I had got the whole picture to a satisfactory state, leaving only the heads relatively unfinished, I had sittings from everyone in turn, including the dog, indoors.

Studies for a family portrait

This is a necessary compromise; it is not really feasible to carry through a painting on this scale entirely in the open air. You need a steadier light. I was lucky to be able to work on this picture in a very light room. It had large windows on two walls, giving a flat, shadowless light on the heads which approximated to an outdoor quality.

The grouping was arrived at by trial and error. As usually happens with a composition of this kind, one or two figures seemed to fall into place straight away and were never moved, except for small alterations of pose; while others were changed again and again. The intention remained the same, however: to give an effect of casual, almost accidental grouping. A lot of hard work can go into getting the right kind of accidental look.

All the figures in a group or double portrait should look as if they have been painted together. This consistency of handling is very difficult to achieve, especially where children are concerned, because one head usually goes better than another; and thus a contrast becomes apparent between a rapidly and freshly painted head, and another which has given trouble and been worked over.

Another point which needs special care is the scale of the heads. It is maddening to get a head right and then find it is just too large or too small in relation to the rest of the picture. Actual heads are very often surprisingly different in size, but though we hardly notice this in ordinary life, it often looks wrong in a picture. Painters like Reynolds and Hals probably evened up the scale of the heads in their groups, making them all roughly the same size.

A double portrait can be a fascinating problem in design. Two rather equal figures are involved, and there is a tendency artificially to make one more important than the other, to avoid the picture falling into two halves. The drawings on the next page show two paintings - by Kokoschka and Van Dyck - in which this problem has not been so much solved as ignored. Both the old and the modern master have accepted the equality of the two figures and have placed them with some symmetry in the long shaped canvas. Neither picture looks in the least as if it could just as well be cut in half to form two portraits; this is largely due to the way the arms and hands have been designed as a link.

Drawing after Kokoschka

Drawing after Van Dyck

9 Varnishing and framing

An oil painting should always be varnished. There are two reasons for doing this. One is protection; the varnish forms a tough layer over the paint which can be handled or cleaned, whereas any unprotected paint surface is liable to damage. The other reason is that oil paint goes matt and dull as it dries; the varnish brings back the freshness that it had when the paint was wet.

The paint must dry out thoroughly before varnishing. It is usual to leave the picture for about nine months. If it has been lying about in the studio for some time, it may be necessary to clean it thoroughly. A liquid detergent will be quite adequate for this purpose. Use a weak dilution in cold water, and go over the surface of the picture with a soft pad soaked in the solution, rubbing lightly. Repeat the process with clean water to remove all traces of detergent, and let the picture dry thoroughly in a warm room.

Varnishing should always be done in a warm, dry atmosphere. If the atmosphere is damp, there is a danger that the varnish will 'bloom' - that is to say, white, milky patches will appear on the surface.

I usually put the varnish, the brush (a fairly soft, wide

one) and the picture in front of a heater for a few minutes to get rid of any damp. Lay the picture face upwards; pour some varnish into a clean tin lid, and brush lightly on. Don't go on brushing backwards and forwards, or you will stir up the varnish into bubbles. If the picture is small, you can brush right across. If it is larger, work across the surface in square areas, completing each square before starting on the next. In either case, try not to disturb the varnish after it has gone on. Your aim should be to get as thin and even a coat as possible. Over-varnishing, with too thick a layer, results in an unpleasantly 'glossy' look.

Arrange the picture so that the light reflects from the wet varnish while you are working; you will then be able to see if you have missed out any small patches. Finally, put the picture to dry, still face up, in a dust-free atmosphere.

A word about retouching varnish. As its name implies, this is a thinned-down varnish used during the course of a picture, or shortly after completion, to bring up dull, 'sunk' passages. It is quite safe to use over half-dry paint, but should not be indulged in to excess. Many people are worried by the natural tendency of oil paint to sink and go dull as it dries. This is more likely to happen if a dark area has been overpainted several times. A point to remember about oil paint is that it always looks fresher when superimposed upon a colour different from itself, particularly in the darks.

Framing

This presents less of a problem than in the past. Nowadays all framers carry a stock of ready-prepared mouldings which can be made up quickly and comparatively cheaply. However, to my mind there is no substitute for a frame which is finished by hand with gesso and real gold leaf in the parts where additional richness is needed. The ready-made variety always has a more meagre appearance, though it is adequate for most purposes. The days are gone when all portraits were put into heavy gold frames; a modern painting in a relatively light key is happier in a light frame, finished perhaps in a greyish neutral colour with gold edges. Many paintings look well with a 'slip' or 'insert' - a thin moulding of light colour - interposed between the picture and the frame.

10 Dealing with commissions

So far we have only touched on the relationship between the painter and his sitter from the point of view of doing as good a painting as possible. When the sitter or someone else is going to buy the picture, the situation becomes more complicated. The painter has to please not only himself, but someone else, or several other people. This can lead to all sorts of compromises. No commission can be called a success unless both parties are reasonably pleased with the result, but one sometimes wonders if any portrait has ever been painted which is admired equally by everyone concerned. There is usually someone who thinks it's terrible.

The difficulty about commissioning a portrait is that, unlike most other work that people order, no one can say how it is going to turn out. It is always to some extent a gamble, and that is the exciting thing about it. So you must make it clear that your client is not bound to accept the picture if he dislikes it. Similarly the artist is not bound to produce a result if he finds the sitter is impossible to paint! You have to risk being left with the portrait on your hands, but take comfort - it has happened before, to artists from Rembrandt to Augustus John. If you are established, you can demand that a proportion of the fee shall be paid even if the portrait is not accepted, but when you are begining to accept commissions you can't very well do more than ask to be reimbursed for your materials.

However, this is perhaps taking too gloomy a view of the situation; it shouldn't often happen that the client really dislikes the result, unless you are a very uncompromising character.

To avoid embarrassment later, settle the fee at the start. Monetary arrangements should never be vague. After you have agreed on the fee, write a letter to the client and get it all in writing. You could put it something like this:
Dear Mr Blank,
This is to confirm that as agreed yesterday I will paint a portrait of your wife. The size is to be . . . . . and the fee . . . . .
It is understood that if you are not satisfied with the result, you are under no obligation to accept it. The fee is not, of

course, inclusive of the frame.

Yours sincerely, etc.

Keep a copy of this letter. You may think all this sounds very formal; I am not suggesting that everyone is out to cheat you, but there is no reason why a portrait commission should be any more vague than any other contract. You don't want to confirm the popular superstition that all painters are unbusinesslike dreamers.

Having a portrait painted is such a personal matter that some people seem embarrassed even to mention a fee. Don't be nervous - name your price boldly, or ask them how much they are prepared to pay, and don't be afraid to bargain. Be prepared at first to work for small fees. It is better to get a steady flow of heads for small fees than to wait years for an expensive one to come along. For one thing, more people will see your work - and in the best possible circumstances; your pictures will look better seen after dinner on the wall of a sitting room than in a mixed exhibition - and also you will feel more free and under less of an obligation to please at all costs if your fees are low. Personal contacts through friends and satisfied customers will probably account for most of your first commissions. To begin with you will probably find yourself painting children rather cheaply, though after doing a few you may come to the conclusion that the nervous strain involved really deserves a higher fee than painting adults! But anyone who gets on well with children and makes a success of painting them is assured of a steady flow of jobs - the number of parents wanting their children painted far outweighs the number of 'boardroom' commissions that are likely to come your way, and there are not all that number of painters who can adapt themselves to the task of painting a lively five year old.

You will often be asked to say how many sittings you will need. Try not to commit yourself. Unless you paint to a formula you can't possibly say. The sitter who keeps asking you how many times more you will need, while you are actually painting, is also to be discouraged. He is rather like the children who say 'Have you finished yet?' after ten minutes work. This sort of thing puts a pressure on the painter. The best sitters feel they are collaborating with the artist in an exciting venture, and not merely coming passively or unwillingly, as if to the dentist. It is to some

A. H. B. Bishop, Esq. (detail)

extent your job to give the sitter this feeling of collaboration.

If possible, a few long sittings are preferable to a number of short ones. You will not necessarily be painting the whole time - quite a lot of your time may be spent in talking to your model and studying him - but you will feel more relaxed. If you only have an hour every Tuesday, there is a tendency to rush things and to feel that every minute of your time has to be spent in 'moving the brush'. I always enjoy a portrait most when I do it either straight off in one go, or in several sittings closely spaced, so that an impetus is kept going. The commissioned portrait of which a detail is shown on this page was done in this way.

I always let the sitter talk. It is possible to carry on a conversation with one level of the mind while concentrating on the painting. If you find that this worries you, try having the radio or record player on while you paint. But conversation, even if intermittent, is preferable, as it is more likely to keep the sitter's face 'alive'.

Another way of keeping the sitter's interest in the whole procedure, and thus ensuring his co-operation, is to let him see the picture as it progresses. Some painters, I know, prefer no one to see their work until it is complete. It is, certainly, easy to be put off by unthinking criticism; but on the other hand, if the sitter can see how his portrait is progressing and how it has changed since last time, he feels more involved, and you avoid that sometimes embarrassing 'moment of truth' when you show him the finished portrait for the first time. You will have to face this confrontation when his family and friends come to see it! Again, I would prefer to let those concerned see the picture before completion. Ask them if they have any criticisms. Someone seeing the picture with a fresh eye may well be able to put their finger on something which has been worrying you. And they will feel that they have contributed a little to the success of the picture.

You will be lucky if everyone is satisfied. Usually there will be some criticisms. If they are minor ones, swallow your pride and make any small modifications you can. But there will come a point when you must say, in effect, 'That's the best I can do, short of repainting the whole thing'. Your clients must understand that continual tinkering in the effort to get the likeness a little more complete is likely to result in more loss than gain. The freshness and unity of the paint can so easily be lost.

The most common criticisms of a portrait are, of course, directed at the expression of the face. 'Something wrong with the mouth', and, 'Too serious (or too old)', are the ones which are likely to recur.

It is fatal to imagine, because you are doing a commissioned portrait, that it is necessary to flatter the sitter. In my experience, few people want to be flattered in a picture, any more than they want it in conversation. Reynolds said that he did not flatter his sitters, but that he did try to show them at their best; this distinction is perhaps worth remembering.

Index